Vostaas
White Buffalo's Story of Plains Indian Life

By William White Buffalo

Recorded by Maxine Ruppel

Illustrated by Students at Labre Indian School
Northern Cheyenne Reservation

Council for Indian Education
2032 Woody Drive
Billings, MT 59102
USA

First edition copyright 1970 under the title
Vostaas: White Buffalo's Story.

ISBN 0-89992-137-X

Acknowledgements
by M. Ruppel

The following people gave unselfishly of their time and effort to assist in the preparation of this material in order to promote a better understanding of American Indian life and culture.

JOHN WOODEN LEGS ("William White Buffalo"), president of the Northern Cheyenne; member of the National Indian Education Advisory Committee

ELIZABETH CLARK, field worker, Association on American Indian Affairs.

DR. HAP GILLILAND, president, Council for Indian Education; director, Reading Center, Eastern Montana College; member, AAIA National Indian Education Committee.

TED RISINGSON

JOE WALKSALONG

ALICE SNODGRASS

JOSEPHINE GLENMORE

BILL WILLIS

Printed in the United States of America
by Quality Press
Englewood, Colorado

To

Patsy
Tony
Daniel
Johnny

The Council for Indian Education

The Council for Indian Education is a non-profit organization devoted to teacher training and to the publication of materials to aid in Native American education. All books are selected for authenticity by an Intertribal Indian Editorial Board and are approved by them for use with Indian children. It is our hope that these books will not only aid in the education of Native children, but will also give non-Indian children a better understanding of their Indian neighbors. All proceeds are used for the publication of more books for Native American children.

Contents

1. White Buffalo's Story 7

2. Who We Are 12
    Early History of the Plains Indians 12
    Names of the Plains Indians 19

3. Where We Live 25
    The Blackfeet Indians 25
    The Crow Indians 26
    The Flathead Indians 27
    The Gros Ventre and Assiniboine Indians 28
    The Assiniboine and Sioux Indians 29
    The Northern Cheyenne Indians 29
    The Cree and Chippewa Indians 31

4. How We Live 33
    Housing 33
    Foods 39

5. What We Do 47
    Education 47
    Religious Beliefs and Practices 51
    Work 54
    Dances and Ceremonies 59

6. What We Hope For 67

Afterword 69

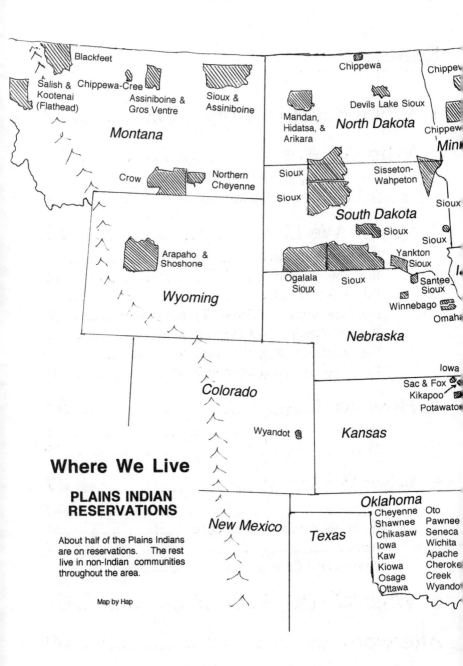

Blackfeet

Salish &
Kootenai
(Flathead)

Chippewa-Cree

Assiniboine &
Gros Ventre

Sioux &
Assiniboine

Montana

Crow

Northern
Cheyenne

Chippewa

Chippew

Devils Lake Sioux

Mandan,
Hidatsa, &
Arikara

North Dakota

Chippew

Min

Sioux

Sioux

Sisseton-
Wahpeton

South Dakota

Sioux

Sioux

Sioux

Yankton
Sioux

Arapaho &
Shoshone

Wyoming

Ogalala
Sioux

Sioux

Santee
Sioux

Winnebago

Omah

Nebraska

Iowa

Sac & Fox

Kikapoo

Potawato

Colorado

Wyandot

Kansas

Where We Live

PLAINS INDIAN
RESERVATIONS

About half of the Plains Indians
are on reservations. The rest
live in non-Indian communities
throughout the area.

Map by Hap

New Mexico

Texas

Oklahoma

Cheyenne   Oto
Shawnee   Pawnee
Chikasaw   Seneca
Iowa   Wichita
Kaw   Apache
Kiowa   Cheroke
Osage   Creek
Ottawa   Wyando

White Buffalo's Story

1

"Indians! Indians!" The bearded scout races toward the wagon train. The wagons are slowly making their way up a beautiful western valley. "Circle your wagons! Get those horses inside!" comes the shout of the wagon boss.

Wagons are soon in place, and barriers are put up in the space between. The scout leaps his horse into the circle of canvas-covered wagons. Rifle muzzles are soon poking out toward the hidden Indians.

G. Fox

Behind a hill a painted medicine man gives the signal. Suddenly, over the horizon appear hundreds of mounted Indian warriors. All are decked out in feathered war bonnets. They carry spears, war clubs, or bows and arrows. With loud war cries, the Indians charge directly at the wagon train. They are soon riding round and round the wagons in a thundering roar of hoofs! There are shots and screams!

But stop! Our TV has shown us again the part of Indian history that we already know. We have seen it over and over on our screens. This is the history of the white settlers' wars against the Indians.

Is this the only part of Indian history that you know? Even the history books you study tell you very little true Indian

history. They tell very little about the way Indians really lived then—or now!

Look around you. Look at your friends, at your classmates. Do they all look alike? Are they all blond or dark-haired? Do they all have the same color of skin? Do they have the same color of eyes?

These are foolish questions, aren't they? Of course we do not all look alike! In the United States there are people of many colors and races. Families may have come from Norway or England or Africa. In fact, a United States family could have come from any nation in the world.

Because your own family came from one certain part of the world, you may be sandy-haired or black-haired. You may have blue, gray, or brown eyes. You may have black or white skin. However you look, you help make up the country that we call the United States.

When you look at the picture on the opposite page I'm sure you say, "There's an Indian!" But how do you know? Because a head dress of feathers means an Indian? Is the picture on this page an Indian, too? This is not so easy to tell, but the picture to the right shows me as I usually look in everyday life. I am an

Indian. I, too, am a citizen of the United States.

My name is William White Buffalo. I have lived all my life in Montana. I am old enough to be a grandfather to several Indian boys and girls. Perhaps one of your classmates is related to me!

Many people talk of Indians as if they lived only in the past. This is far from true. There are about 48,000 American Indians in Montana. Oklahoma, South Dakota, and North Dakota are other Plains area states with many Indian people. But there are a lot of Indians in every state. In fact, there are about two million Indians in the United States as a whole. Probably some of your schoolmates whom you never thought of as Indians are at least partly Indian.

How many true things do you know about these Indians and their ways? Many boys and girls know about Indians only from TV or movies. I have written this book because I want to tell you things about my people that are really true.

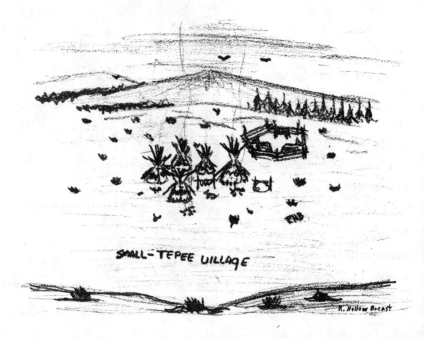

SMALL-TEPEE VILLAGE

I will tell you about my own family and how we live. I will tell you about the deep love the Indian people have for their lands. I will tell you about some of my friends who have left the reservation to work in other places. I will tell you about some of my people who have stayed on the reservation.

I will tell you about some of the old ways of the Indians, when my people lived in tipis, when they hunted buffalo and other game, when they raced their horses with the wind and there were no fences or plowed fields to stop them.

From these old times come the stories about Indians you have seen on television. We Indians laugh and sometimes grow very angry at the way the Indian people are made to appear on TV. Perhaps as you read you will understand more about Indians, about our old ways . . . and our "new" ways.

Much of what I tell you will be about Montana Indians, but you should remember that the way of life of most Plains Indians is and was much alike, so almost all of what I say will apply to nearly all Indians of the plains. Remember too, however, that each group of Indians has some customs and traditions that are different from any of the others. After you have read this book, you should try to learn more about your own people, or the Indian people who live nearest to you.

I hope that, as you understand Indians better, you will see why Indian people, as they adopt some of the white man's ways, would also like to keep some of their Indian ways.

Who We Are

2

Early History of the Plains Indians

Why we are called Indians

Christopher Columbus made a mistake when he landed his boats on the shores of the new land! He thought the world was much smaller than it really is, so he thought he had sailed all the way around it and had landed in India. That is why he called the brown skinned people he saw "Indians." By the time he found out these people did not live in India, everyone was calling them "Indians," and the name has never changed.

Columbus did not know it, but there were many different groups or nations of these brown-skinned people. They spoke many different languages. They had many different ways of living. They had many different ways of building houses and of making clothing. Yet, all of these groups of people are now called "Indians" because one man made a mistake!

Nowadays, we are used to being called Indians. However, as more people travel around the world and meet the Indians of India, the name *Indian* can become confusing. Therefore, many of our people much prefer to be called Native Americans. For this book, when we want to refer to all Native Americans as a group, we will use the title American Indians because that is the name by which most of our readers know us.

Still, all of us, whom you might call Indians or Native Americans, would really prefer to be called by the name of our group. We like to be called Mohawks, Cherokees, Apaches, Navajo, Blackfeet, Cheyenne, or Pima, just as people who are German, French or Italian would prefer to be called by those names rather than just "Europeans." These are the names that really tell who we are. But we *all* like to be called Americans, don't we?

My own people are the Northern Cheyennes. The Northern Cheyennes live in the south-central part of Montana. We have some land called a "reservation." There are seven such reservations in Montana, and many more in other parts of the West. My life among my own people is much like life among any of the Plains Indians.

In the old days the Plains Indians rode horses. They wore eagle feather headdresses. They lived in tipis. They hunted the buffalo.

The Indians you see on TV and in the movies are nearly always Plains Indians. Most of Montana's Indians were classed as Indians of the Plains. These plains are that great land between the Rocky Mountains and the Mississippi River. They stretch from Canada in the north to Texas in the south.

How did the Indians come to live on the plains? Why is it that all over the world, when people think of Indians, they think of the Plains Indians?

Where the Plains Indians came from

To begin to tell about Plains Indian history, I must take you to the southwestern part of our United States.

The great explorers from Spain had a lot to do with our story about Indians. How could that be? It is very simple. The Spanish explorers had horses.

Horses were unknown on the North American continent up to the time the Spanish people arrived in the 1500's. Not one Indian in the North or South American continents had ever ridden a horse. Not one Indian had even seen a horse! When the Indians saw horses, they were afraid of them. It did not take long, though, for the Indians to get over their fear. They began to see that it would be very good to have horses of their own.

The Spanish explorers didn't want the Indians to have horses. But as horses do, some broke loose. They began to drift to the north. Soon great herds of horses were grazing on the plains. The Indians learned to capture and tame them. Probably nothing changed the life of the Indians as much as having horses did.

When the horses first began spreading northward, most of the ancestors of our Northern Plains Indians were wandering gatherers or planters of crops. They were living in what are now Minnesota and Wisconsin and parts of eastern Canada.

There were also tribes like the Flatheads who lived west of the Rocky Mountains. Sometimes hunting parties from either the mountains on the west or from the woodlands east of the plains would come to the plains on foot to drive buffalo over the cliffs. These buffalo hunts furnished meat for the winters. The Indians would then make the long trip back home, carrying the meat with them.

Meanwhile there was trouble further east. Indian tribes who had once lived along the Atlantic coast were being driven westward by the white settlers. These Indians were driving weaker tribes west to the plains.

Perhaps this was good luck for my ancestors! It was about this time that they got horses from southern tribes. They and members of other tribes driven from Minnesota, Wisconsin and Canada began to develop the great culture, or way of life, of the Plains Indian. This culture was centered on buffalo and horses. A way of life was built around both animals.

Wm Poser

It is from this time in history that people all over the world form their picture of the American Indians. They know about the horses, beaded costumes, bows and arrows, tipis, skin clothing, and feathered headdresses. Book writers, movie makers, and now TV actors all show us how the Plains Indian lived his free, good life. Of course, many of these books and shows are not true to the way the Indians really lived, but the old way of life was for the Indians a "time of glory."

What changed the Plains Indians' way of life

What happened to the Plains Indians? What changed their way of life? The answer to these questions is a sad story in the history of our country and especially for the native peoples of the plains.

Captain William Clark and Meriwether Lewis were sent out by President Jefferson in 1804 to explore the Louisiana Territory. The Indians they met along the way were mostly friendly. Many of the Indian people helped the explorers get food and horses. Many of the Indian warriors were able to help the white men locate rivers and mountain passes.

When returning through Montana, Lewis had a misunderstanding with a small band of Blackfeet. One Indian was killed. It is possible that this one death began the Blackfeet's hatred of the white men. If a group of strange-looking men came into  your neighborhood and killed one of your friends, would you not hate the stranger?

Clark returned along the Yellowstone River. He lost some horses, probably to Crow Indian raiders.

These two events were the only real troubles with Indians that the two explorers had.

When the story of Lewis and Clark and the wonderful country they had explored reached the states east of the Mississippi River, white people began to look westward to the great plains, rivers, and mountains. Slowly at first, but in ever growing numbers, they began to move into the open hunting lands of the Indians. When gold was discovered in Montana, white people came from all directions to dig for that precious metal.

Can you imagine what it was like for the Indians to see hundreds and hundreds of white men, women, and children moving onto the land that was their valuable hunting grounds? The buffalo began to disappear. Steamboats with

their black smoke began to steam up the large rivers. Cattle herds moved into the buffalo range. Plows began to "turn the grass upside down," as the Indians explained it. Maybe worst of all, the "Yellowlegs," the United States Cavalry, came along to protect the white settlers from the Indians.

What did the Indians do about this invasion? They could do just one thing. They tried to protect their land. They tried to drive the white settlers out by force. There were battles. There were successful raids by Indians against white settlements. Sometimes for a year or two a treaty would keep white settlers off the hunting grounds. Treaties were made; treaties were broken. The Indians were forced into smaller and smaller territories. Eventually, certain lands were set aside for them. Usually these lands were the poorest left after the white men got what they wanted. The Indians were told they must live, somehow, on these poor lands. The lands were to be called "reservations."

The last big battle on the plains was in 1876 on the Little Big Horn River. General George Custer and 300 of his men attacked a large encampment of Sioux and Northern Chey-

18

enne. These people sent out their warriors to protect them, and all of Custer's men were killed.

The Little Big Horn battle was a short victory for the Indians, though. The United States government and Army promised to wipe out every warring nation among the Indians. In a few years, the force of the Indians was broken forever. The great warriors who were trying to protect their homeland were either dead or placed in captivity on the reservations.

Names of the Plains Indians

Indian names aren't that different!

Sometimes people who do not understand Indian names make fun of Indian names they hear. Sometimes Indian people have changed their names to "white" names so they won't be laughed at. However, Indian names are names to be proud of. Many Indians have names that were given to their ancestors because of brave deeds or great accomplishments.

Indian names are really much like the names of most of your friends. If you look in most phone books in the United States you will find the name "Farmer." How did the person get that name? Because long ago a man who was a farmer took that name. Other names also show the work a man did: Carpenter, Bowman, Smith (for blacksmith). Some names were once the names of places: Fields, Woods, Hill, House, and Lake are five examples. Some names were taken from the animal world—Fox, Swan, Wolf, and even Worm. Some names were names of qualities: Hardy, Young, Olds, Friend. Davidson means "son of David." Peterson means "son of Peter." Norlander means a man from the Northland. These are the easy names.

What about names like Wyrzkowski, Zickefoose, Stelma-chuk, or Substyk? These names, too, would be names of things similar to Indian names if you knew the languages from which they came. Do you have friends who are Polish, Russian, or French? Have you ever asked them what their names mean?

Perhaps you can find the history of your own name. Look in a big dictionary, or ask your librarian.

Personal names

An Indian of the past did not keep one name all his life. One Indian might have many different names. An Indian baby would be named a pet name, usually by his mother. One of my grandfathers was called "Eats From His Hand" when he was a baby. He was called that name until he was about 14 years old. Then he was called "Lame Buffalo" from a dream he had. As he grew taller and taller, he was called "Tall Man" by his friends. Finally, he earned his warrior's name, which was "Wooden Legs." He got this name because he had great strength in his legs. His legs seemed never to get tired. Finally, when grandfather was an old man, he was called "Goat Whiskers," because he had a few long hairs on his chin.

I can remember my grandmother calling "Goat Whiskers" to a meal. When she was angry at him for not coming right away, she would call him by all five of his names!

Indian women did not change names as often as men did. If a woman was a medicine woman or performed some especially brave deed, she might earn a name for herself. Often, though, women went through life with just one name.

All members of an Indian family did not have the same name. Husbands and wives had different names, as did each of their children. A name was not passed down from father to son, although at special ceremonies a father's famous name might be given to another young man. In that case, the father would take a new name and never again use the one he had given away.

Men and women sometimes got names from something they did, or from something that happened to them. Their names might tell the kind of person they were. What kind of person would have these Indian names: Crooked Foot, Falling-Down Woman, Straight Arrow, Runs-Away-With-His-Horses, Black Eagle Feather, Left-Hand-Tied-Behind, or Red-Colored Corn Woman?

Indian names often do not have the same meaning when they are translated into English. Dirty Face is a good Indian name. You may think of someone with a very dirty face when you hear that name, but the name in Indian had nothing to do with dirt. It really is the name of a famous warrior, but the meaning changed when it was translated because there was no English word that would mean "A man who has a very fierce look on his face when he goes into battle." Yellow Belly is another good Indian name. It was given to a man who liked to use yellow war paint on his body.

Family names

When the Indians were first brought in to the reservations, the United States government tried to make a list of all the Indians. These Indian people had never had their names written before. They did not speak English, and their language had never been put into writing. They knew a lot of their own history, but it was not written down. It was memorized and kept in the heads of the old and wise men and women.

When the government wanted a list of all of the Indians, my family went together to have their names written on the list. My great-grandfather was first, since he was the head of the family. His name was Vostaas in Northern Cheyenne. An interpreter said, "This man's name is White Buffalo." My great-grandmother's name was written as Mrs. White Buffalo, although that was not her name at all. The children were called next, and they were all recorded as members of the White Buffalo family, although as we know, each Indian child had his own name. One of these children grew up and became my grandfather. Now I am known as William White Buffalo. My son is called Nelson White Buffalo, and my daughter is called Linda White Buffalo. We now give our own children first names taken from the white man, and use our Indian family name.

Even though we have an official name on the school lists, most of us still have an Indian name in our own language. Sometimes we take our Indian names for ourselves. Sometimes they are given to us by a friend, relative, or our parents. An Indian soldier might be given a special warrior name when he returns from the Army. I also have such a special name. It is a famous warrior name. In the Northern Cheyenne language it is written *Homa'ox Moxtavastse*. This name is translated "Black Beaver" in English.

Perhaps now the Indian names you may see or hear will not seem so strange. There is a story behind every Indian name, just as there is a story to almost every name in every language. We should all be proud of our names.

Indian names today

Not all Indian names have been translated into English. Some Indians still use a name in their Indian language. When you say their names you are speaking an Indian language. There are many other things that we call by their Indian names. This includes many of our states. Here is a list of some of the states that have Indian names. There are others. Say these out loud. You are speaking an Indian language!

Massachusetts	Dakota	Alaska
Delaware	Iowa	Michigan
Wisconsin	Ohio	Utah
Mississippi	Alabama	Oklahoma
Tennessee	Missouri	Minnesota

The names of hundreds of towns and rivers are Indian names. Many other things are also known by their Indian names. Squash, cucumber, pumpkin, and tomato are Indian names for foods that were first grown by the Indians and were unknown to the rest of the world until the first Europeans came to America.

There are still many Indian people who are fluent in both English and their own language. Some of them—for instance, most Navajo and Hopi children who live on reservations— speak their people's languages at home. Most Crow children, too, are fluent in their own language. Some of these children do not learn English until they start school. The only time they use English is while they are at school. The Cheyenne, Sioux, and Blackfeet children of 25 years ago learned their people's language first, but now nearly all of them are more fluent in English than in their own language. Most of the other Plains Indian children know very little of their native languages. In fact, most Indians throughout the U.S. speak only English.

More and more elders in many tribes feel badly that their children are not learning their own languages. These elders want the children to recognize the value of their culture and the value of their people's heritage, so they are working hard to help the children of their tribes to learn their own languages. None of them expect their people to use their native languages *instead of* English, but they do hope their people will use their languages *with* English.

Because languages and cultures develop together, it is usually far easier to express one's deepest thoughts and feelings in one's own language rather than in another language.

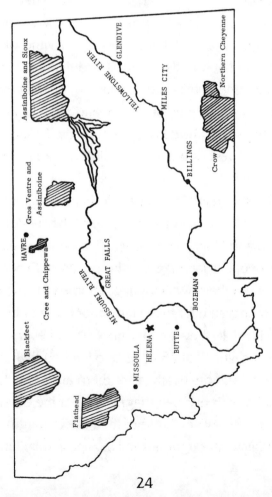

Where We Live

3

On the opposite page is a map of Montana. Seven Montana Indian reservations are shown on this map. Back on page 6 is another map that shows the reservations in all of the Plains states so you can locate the places that many Indian peoples call home. A different group, or "tribe," of Indians lives on each of these reservations. A "reservation" is land that was "reserved" for the use of the Indians, so the settlers could not take all of the land that once belonged to the Indians.

More than half of the Indians in Montana live on reservations, but many also live in Billings, Great Falls, and in smaller towns.

In many ways the different groups of Plains Indians were alike, and yet in other ways they were very different. Find the location of each reservation on the map as you read about the different groups of Indians.

The Blackfeet Indians

The Blackfeet Indians have a reservation that is east of Glacier Park and just south of the Canadian border. About half of all the Blackfeet Indians still live on this reservation.

There are no records of the origin of their name, but there is a story that says that when the first white men in the area met the Blackfeet Indians, they had been walking across land that had just been burned by a prairie fire. Their moccasins were black from the ashes, so the white men called them "Blackfeet."

The Blackfeet moved into Montana early in the 1700's from Canada. It was also about this time that they first obtained horses. They were looking for better hunting grounds, and after they got some horses, they became great hunters. They also developed into famous warriors and horsemen.

The Blackfeet people were never friendly to white Americans. They made war on all intruders, Indian or white.

The United States Army, along with outbreaks of disease, combined to force the Blackfeet people to surrender to reservation life. Since that time, the Blackfeet people have struggled for existence.

Only lately have agriculture and cattle-raising become successful. Oil discovered on reservation lands has brought some money to the people. Industries are now being invited to open small factories on the Blackfeet land.

The bead and leather work of the Blackfeet women is very famous. It is sold in a shop in Browning, Montana, as well as in other places.

The Crow Indians

Near the southern edge of Montana are two reservations with a single boundary between them. Of these two, the larger belongs to the "Absarokee" Indians, or Crows. They got the name Crow from the white men who saw the sign used for them. Their sign involved flapping their arms to indicate bird's wings.

The Crows have a history of friendliness to the white men. They hoped that the whites would help them against their Indian enemies.

The Crow reservation is within what was once part of their hunting grounds. It was once much larger than it is now, and included much of the Yellowstone River Valley. There is good farm land along the Big Horn River. Much of the land is irrigated. Most of this land, however, is rented out to white farmers. Many of the Crow people suffer from lack of steady work.

Three tourist attractions are found on the Crow reservation. One is the Custer Battlefield. General Custer and his men were attacked and wiped out by Cheyenne and Sioux Indians at this place in 1876. Custer had some Crow Indians with him as scouts. Now the Custer Battlefield is a National Cemetery and Monument. It is visited by thousands of tourists each year.

Another tourist attraction is Yellowtail Dam. Here a giant lake backs up behind the dam on the Big Horn River. The Crow Indians hope to develop places for recreation around the lake shores.

The third tourist attraction is the home of Plenty Coups, the last of the great chiefs of the Crows. After his death his home near Pryor was made into a museum. The Crows have a park and campground near this museum.

New homes can be seen in many parts of the Crow reservation. These homes were built under a "family plan." Each person in the tribe was allowed $1,000 from a government payment for lands taken away from the Crows in early days. This money had to be used for useful things. Many families built new homes.

There are some oil wells on the Crow reservation. Small industries furnish some jobs to Crow men and women.

The Flathead Indians

The Flathead Indians live in some of Montana's most beautiful mountain country. Their reservation includes Flathead Lake.

These people area part of the Salish-Kootenai Indian groups. They got the name of Flathead from the coast Indians, who lived to the west of them. The coast Indians made the heads of their babies grow longer by pressing and binding a board to their foreheads. This caused the heads to grow long and pointed. To the people with long heads, the heads of their neighbors looked flat, so they called them Flatheads.

The Flatheads were once great fish eaters. After the coming of the horses, however, they began to hunt buffalo. There were few buffalo in their own lands, so once a year they would go over the mountains to the Blackfeet hunting grounds. Here they would hunt buffalo. It was very dangerous for the Flatheads to hunt buffalo since the Blackfeet Indians did not like to have other hunters on their lands.

When the Flatheads came into contact with the Plains Indians they took some of their ways. However, they have always been more like the Indians of the Northwest than the Plains Indians.

The Flatheads have gained money and jobs from the sale of timber from their reservation. They operate resort areas on Flathead Lake. They also receive money in rent from the Montana Power Company for the use of Kerr Dam.

The Gros Ventre and Assiniboine Indians

On your reference map, locate the Fort Belknap Reservation. It is in north-central Montana from the Milk River to the Little Rockies. This land is shared by members of the Gros Ventre and Assiniboine groups.

These groups were once terrible enemies but now share a small bit of Montana's land. Because the two groups spoke different languages, they learned to speak English to each other. There is little of their Indian language used now.

Some of the people live on farms and ranches. Some of the grazing land is rented to white cattlemen.

Mission Canyon, in the Little Rocky Mountains, is a tourist attraction. The Fort Belknap Indians have a public campground there.

The Assiniboine and Sioux Indians

Near the northeast corner of Montana is the Fort Peck Reservation. There are many Sioux Indians there, although the Assiniboine were first to live and hunt in this area. Some bands of Sioux joined them to receive government food rations about the year 1872. Since that time, the two groups have shared the Fort Peck Reservation. Most of the Sioux Indians, however, live on reservations in North and South Dakota.

Conditions on this reservation are very poor, and there are few jobs for anyone. Some irrigation projects are being developed. There is some money from oil. The Indian government tries to encourage ranching by Indians themselves. Some new houses are being built, but the people need jobs for year-around money.

The Northern Cheyenne Indians

All of the Cheyenne Indians once lived in the farming regions of Minnesota and Wisconsin. They raised corn and other crops. They made clay pottery. Just before 1700, however, they were driven west by the movement of eastern tribes. On the plains, the Cheyennes became great hunters.

When they obtained horses, they became fierce warriors and made war on many other Indian groups.

Sometime before 1850 the Cheyennes split into two groups, Northern and Southern. When the white men invaded their land, the Southern Cheyennes moved to Oklahoma. The Northern Cheyennes stayed on the northern plains.

They joined the Sioux Indians to make war on the white invaders. With the Sioux, they wiped out Custer's men at the Battle of the Little Big Horn.

Soon after this, the Army forced the men, women, and children of the Northern Cheyennes to move to Oklahoma. In the hot climate of Oklahoma, many of these people died of disease and homesickness. In order to save their people, two of the Indian leaders decided to break away and lead the way back to the plains. These two leaders were Little Wolf and Dull Knife. Not many of the Northern Cheyennes lived to get back to the plains because it was winter and the Army was chasing them. The Indians fought nearly all of the long way home. Many of the people were killed. Others died of starvation and cold.

The struggle of the Northern Cheyennes to reach the plains did convince the United States government that a reservation should be set aside for them. Finally they were given a small reservation of their own. It is in southern Montana and shares a border with the Crow reservation.

The Northern Cheyennes have taken The Morning Star People as a new name. The morning star has always been a special star to the Cheyennes. It has a special name in their language. That name is WO HE HIV. The star tells the Cheyennes that with the coming of each new day, there is new life and hope.

The Northern Cheyenne reservation is small. The people have been very poor for many years. Now the Morning Star People are looking for new ways to help themselves.

Sale of timber, coal, and cattle are means of raising money. Some people work in small industries, schools, and in government jobs.

The Northern Cheyennes operate a store at Lame Deer where beaded work is sold. Tourists may rent a tipi for overnight. There are several campgrounds for travelers.

The Cree and Chippewa Indians

The smallest reservation in Montana is Rocky Boy's reservation. It also has the smallest number of Indians living on it. The land was set aside to give some very poor wandering bands of Cree and Chippewa Indians a home.

The name of the reservation and its people was taken from the name of a Chippewa leader, Stone Child. The white men called him Rocky Boy, and when these Indians obtained a reservation, they called it "Rocky Boy's Reservation."

The Rocky Boy's Reservation is very poor. Hay land is its main resource; cattle grazing is the main source of income. Most of the Indian families move away from their homes during the summer months to take jobs. During the winter there is little money for the people.

Some money comes from renting grazing lands to white ranchers. The Cree and Chippewa who remain on the reservation hope to be able to attract tourists to their land.

*****

Even though all these Indian reservations have many things to overcome, much is happening today to bring a better life to the people who live there.

31

Our government, both federal and state, is giving many kinds of help. This includes loans or grants of money to build better houses, better schools, and buildings for small industries where people can have jobs. It includes different kinds of training to help people get better jobs. It means getting water and sewers for houses that never had these.

Private groups, churches, colleges, and universities offer help to Indian reservations too.

Because of all this interest and help, life is getting better for many Indian people. The future looks brighter than it has for many years in the past.

How We Live

4

Housing

In Montana and in other states, many people like to camp in the mountains and by the streams. These people carry tents to set up. Sometimes they drive campers and trailers into the campgrounds. Whatever shelter they use to live in, people seem to like to travel from place to place and to carry their own movable homes with them. They like to see new scenes, visit tourist attractions, and to meet new people. They like to take in sports events, go fishing, swim, or just enjoy the out-of-doors.

The Tipi: America's First Mobile Home

What you have just read also describes how the Indian people of Montana lived years ago. They moved from place to place, not on wheels but on horseback. They moved their homes along with them. These first mobile homes were called "tipis." Indians enjoyed the change of scenery. They enjoyed visiting with friends and relatives. However, they did not always move for reasons of pleasure. The most important reasons for moving were to find new hunting grounds and to find fresh grass for their horses.

Can you imagine how wonderful it was for the Indian people to start out across the country to the distant mountains and not have to follow highways or stop for fences? It was because they were used to moving around freely that the

Indians found it so hard to stay on reservations. They were not used to looking at lines drawn on a map, especially when these lines meant they could not go outside the boundary lines.

Actually, the free life of the Plains Indians lasted a short time in history. But the tipis that my people once used with such pride have become a common symbol of Indians. I have seen drawings of the Pilgrims landing on the shores of North America, and on that land are shown tipis of the Indians!

Truthfully, only the Indians of the Plains used tipis. Indian people of other parts of North America used other kinds of shelters. They used bark wigwams, earth lodges, log hogans, and houses made of reeds and grasses. Plains Indians made tipis that were easy to move, and these tipis became the first "mobile homes."

Barbara S.

How Tipis Were Made

We don't really know how tipis were first made. Probably the idea came from some simple shelter made from a buffalo hide thrown over a few sticks. During the greatest time of the Plains Indians, the tipis were made of long poles carefully fitted together at the top. The poles were spread in a large circle at the bottom. Buffalo hides sewn together by the women were laid over the poles. These tipis were cool in the summer and warm in the winter.

Sometimes the tipis were painted in bright colors, but they were often left in the natural color of the hides. All tipis that were used by the families turned dark around the top from fire smoke escaping through the hole at the peak.

When the man of a family was home, a good horse was often tied at the front of the tipi. Some of the man's weapons or other objects of value were hung outside the flap that served as a door.

In good weather the women cooked out-of-doors. When the weather was bad, they cooked inside the tipi. They would build a fire in the middle of the tipi's circle and the family stayed warm and comfortable. There would be buffalo robes to lie on and to use as coverings.

How inviting the night camp must have looked to a returning war party! They would be able to see the glow of the tipis from the distance and smell the wood smoke curling from their peaks!

When it was time for the camp to be moved, the women packed the belongings of the family in rawhide bags. They took down the hide coverings and poles. They arranged the poles on gentle horses so that the ends of the poles could drag on the ground on either side of the horses. Bundles of belongings would be tied to the poles on strips of hide slung between the poles. This drag was called a *travois* (truh-VWAH). You can see by the picture that this made a good place for young children to ride!

The Indian people enjoyed moving to new places. There was singing, joking, and much talking among the people as they moved. Young boys drove the horse herds. The men rode at the front, sides, and rear to protect the women and children. The group would stop and set up camp whenever the scouts found a good place where there was water, wood, and the promise of good hunting. Each tipi had its own place, and they were always set up with the doors facing east.

Fixed housing

Now my story becomes quite sad. This wonderful life was to be no more, ever again. The Indian people had to change their way of living when the buffalo were all gone. They had to learn to stay on one little plot of land instead of roaming freely.

When my people were forced to go to the reservation, many of the tipis were destroyed by the Army. Those tipis that remained began to wear out. There were no more buffalo hides to be found. If tipis were made at all, they were made of canvas, although a canvas tipi is not very warm!

What did the Indian people do as their tipis wore out? Some of them got large wall tents from the Army and lived in these. However, now that they were on reservations, the families were not able to move their homes as they had always done. The ground around the tents was soon beaten down until there was only dust in summer and mud when the rain or snow fell. The tents soon became very dirty.

Some of the people tried to build houses, but they knew nothing about building. They tried to build log houses. These were usually very small so they could be kept warm in the winters. Often many people would live together in these small places. The people could not stand the crowding and the dirt. Soon the Indians caught many of the white man's diseases. Many Indians died as a result.

Even now, if you should drive through any of our Montana reservations, you will see small log houses and shacks where Indian people live. You would probably say, "I wouldn't want to live that way!"

This is what the Indian people say, too. At last it is becoming possible for Indian families to get better houses, but for many years there were no nice homes on the reservations. Even the few Indians who had good jobs could not save enough money to build houses.

When people in the cities want to build houses, they borrow the money. They build the house and pay for it while they live in it. On the reservations, however, the land belonged to the tribe, so the banks could not loan money so that Indians could build their own homes. Now the government has worked out ways in which Indians can get help to improve their housing.

Indian homes today

Some of the new homes on the reservations are prefabricated. This means that they are all ready to put up, wall by wall. The houses are shipped in on a truck, and men put them up by following directions. Others of the new homes are of new logs. These log homes are larger than the shacks that were once built. They are warm and clean.

We are proud of our new homes. In our towns we now have streets and alleys. New water systems bring clean water to the kitchens of the new homes. Water is no longer carried bucket by bucket from a common well.

Many Indian people still burn wood in their stoves because gas or oil for stoves is very expensive. Many Indian boys, and some girls, too, learn to chop wood when they are quite young! Our mothers do not say, "No! No! That axe is too sharp for you to use!" They say, "Go chop some more wood. Is the axe sharp enough?"

Some of my people have learned to plant grass, flowers, and trees around their new homes. Like most Indians, my family likes the out-of-doors, and we may put up a brush shelter over our lawn during the summer. Under its shade, we do some of our cooking and eating. White people would call this a patio! It is very pleasant in the shade, and we like to have friends join us there. We usually put up a tent in the summer, too, so the family and friends may use it.

When I look about me, I feel very sad to see some of my people still living in old, cold shacks. Many are still crowded together in one or two little rooms. Not all of them keep warm in the winters.

I talk with young Indian men and women. We plan on what we can do to make things better for ourselves and our families. I know that one day the old shacks will all be gone. The Indian people will build more new homes. They will build a new life for themselves, along with the new homes.

Foods

Buffalo

"Buffalo sighted! Buffalo sighted! Meat for all!"

A scout rides into the Indian camp and announces to the leaders of the group that he has located a buffalo herd. The leaders quickly meet to plan the best way to attack the herd so that the most animals can be killed. It is important to make careful plans so that the herd will not be frightened away too soon. Since these people of the Plains are skilled at hunting buffalo, a plan is soon made and word is sent to the hunters to get ready.

The horse herders drive the horses in from where they have been grazing. The women catch their pack horses. The hunters mount their best buffalo horses—horses that are especially strong and swift and are not afraid to run in close to a stampeding herd of mighty buffalo.

The men are armed mostly with bows and arrows. Even if they own guns, they prefer the old weapons because they are quiet and do not frighten the buffalo herd.

Scouts lead the hunting party toward the great herds of buffalo. The herd is moving toward the distant river.

The hunters range themselves downwind from the buffalo. Each man waits for the signal to attack. The herd must not be frightened before all are ready. At a signal, the men ride toward the herd. Each hunter tries to ride near to the side of a buffalo. He wants to sink an arrow into a vital spot before the animals become alarmed and begin to run. Soon, though, all is dust and thundering hoofs and the buffalo sense danger all about them. The horses of the hunters begin to run hard alongside the bellowing buffalo bulls and cows in order to carry the men close enough for a clean kill.

If the hunters are skilled and the arrows are sharp, enough

buffalo are soon killed to furnish meat for the camp for a long time. The hunters turn their weary horses back, but the buffalo herd will rumble on for miles before it stops running.

Now the real work begins, but there are smiles on the faces of the women and children and old people. They come up to begin skinning the dead animals. They cut up the meat to pack it back to camp. Every part of the buffalo is saved for some special use.

By nightfall, there is little left on the prairie for the coyotes to clean up. The mouth-watering odors of roasting ribs, hump meat, and tongue come from every fire in the camp. Everyone eats until he can hold no more. Meat is shared by the whole camp. Soup is prepared for the sick or the very old. No one goes hungry.

The next day, the women begin tanning buffalo hides. Meat is hung up on racks to dry. It will be stored for winter use.

I myself have heard and read much about these great buffalo hunts. My grandfather often told of his experiences hunting buffalo and the feasts that followed. As I write about the feasts, I can almost taste the good meat.

In these times, there are some buffalo left because there are herds of the animals raised on some of the reservations. Sometimes a buffalo is killed for a special occasion and many of us get a taste of buffalo meat.

When the Buffalo Disappeared

It was when they noticed that the buffalo were disappearing that the Indian people in Montana became alarmed about the number of white men who were coming into their hunting grounds. White hunters killed many buffalo only for their hides. They shot hundreds of thousands of buffalo and left the good meat rotting on the ground. Soon—it seemed almost overnight—the Indian people could find no living buffalo left to eat, to furnish hides for tipis, or to make robes for the cold winters.

This was a very bad time. Many of the Indian people starved before the government of the United States realized that they were starving. The Plains Indians did not know how to get food any way but by hunting—and there was nothing left to hunt.

Preserved meats

Sometimes there were many animals to kill. Sometimes you could go for days or even weeks without finding a single deer or buffalo. To take care of these lean times, the Indians made most of their meat into jerky and pemmican which would keep all winter without spoiling. By using these methods of preserving meat, a good buffalo hunt could furnish food enough to last a long time.

Jerky

Jerky is a popular food with many people. It is one Indian food that you can buy in some stores. It is very expensive to buy, but it is not hard to make your own. Many Indian families still go deer hunting and make the meat into jerky to eat during the winter.

If you want to make some jerky, you will first need a very sharp knife and a chunk of lean beef or deer meat. Look closely at your piece of meat. You will see it has a grain, almost like a piece of wood has. Cut long thin strips of meat *with* the grain of the meat. The strips must be thin, and they must be with the grain, or they will fall apart as they dry.

After the strips are cut, put a little salt on each side of each strip. Hang the strips on a string to dry. If the weather is warm and dry, the meat can be hung outside, and it will dry quickly. If you do hang it outside, though, be sure the dogs cannot reach it, as dogs love jerky, too!

If the weather is damp, you can dry your jerky in an oven. Set the oven so it will stay about 140 to 150 degrees. Be sure it is not too hot. Lay the strips of meat on the racks next to each other so that they can dry well. Leave them in the oven about 24 hours. Once the jerky is completely dry, it will keep as long as you and your family can keep from eating it!

Pemmican

Another food that the Indian people used during the winters was pemmican. Pemmican was such a good food and kept so well that many of the early white men learned to make it, or bought it, or stole it! The United States Army still sends a kind of pemmican with the men who must be away from their food supply, because pemmican is a very concentrated food. A small amount will supply a man with food for a long time. In the old days, when a man was going on a long hunting trip, a small bag of pemmican and some strips of jerky were usually the only food he took.

You can make pemmican, too, if you have made jerky first.

During the late summer season, go out and gather chokecherries. If you cannot find these, you may use raisins, dried cranberries, or currants for your fruit.

If you are using chokecherries, crush the fruit by pounding it (or, if you prefer, use a food grinder!), then dry the pieces in the sun. When the fruit has dried thoroughly, pound or grind up a supply of jerky, as well, then mix the fruit and jerky with a small amount of melted fat or tallow to hold them together. This pemmican can be safely stored for a long time. To the Indians, the fruit in the pemmican acts as a kind of vitamin pill during the long winter months.

New foods

The Indian people have had to learn to eat the food of the white men. Since there were no words in their language for many of the unfamiliar foods, words were made up to describe the foods. To us, today, these words sometimes sound very funny! Here are a few samples.

Coffee—black soup
Oatmeal—slobbering gravy
Banana—crooked neck apple
Pear—sharp pointed apple
Orange—yellow apple

You can tell from the names above that the Indian people had a word for apple because they knew that fruit—but then all other fruits became different kinds of "apples"!

Nowadays, in most of our reservation towns, or in towns nearby, Indian people can shop in supermarkets, just as you do. We have refrigerators in our homes. Our young girls are trained in high school classes how to choose foods for good health. Many of our women cook foods much as all mothers do.

Favorite foods

Like most people, we Indian people like to gather together with our friends to eat and to visit. At these gatherings our meals will include a feast of boiled deer meat or beef, sometimes with potatoes, onions, or other vegetables. We also enjoy canned fruit, coffee, and lots of fried bread. When they are ripe, many of us gather June berries, chokecherries, buffalo berries, and wild plums.

The Indian women make fried bread, sometimes called grease bread. It is something everyone likes! Many of our white friends beg our women to make fried bread for them! When the Indian people first were given flour, they did not know how to use it, but they soon developed a way to use flour: that is the fried bread we eat now.

Here is a recipe for fried bread that you can try at home. Be sure you are especially careful with the hot fat so you won't get burned.

Mix together the following ingredients:

2 cups flour	$^1/_2$ cup dried milk
1 tsp. salt	1 tbsp sugar
2 tsp. baking powder	About 1 cup warm water

On a floured board, pat the dough into 8"-9" circles about $^1/_2$" thick. Cut into pie shaped wedges. Cut a little slit in the center of each. Fry quickly in hot fat until nicely browned. Fat should be just below the smoking point.

Food for everyone

One of the most valuable possessions an Indian family could have was a supply of pemmican and jerky stored in rawhide bags. The men who were good hunters and the women who could make a good supply of winter food were the admired members of the Indian camps. These people knew they were admired and would share their skills and food with other members of their group.

As long as there was food in the camp, no one starved. The food was used for the good of all. Sometimes, when hunting was bad, no one had enough to eat. When one person was hungry, it was likely that all people in the camp were hungry, because they shared whatever little that they had. When there was plenty of meat, everyone ate well. The old people, the crippled, the orphans, the widows—all shared in the common food supply.

In modern times on the reservation, this old custom of sharing has not died out. As long as there is any food at all, it is shared with those less able to take care of themselves. I don't know one of my friends who, when he kills an elk, deer, or antelope, keeps more than a fourth of the meat for himself. He gives most of it away to friends and family. He wants it to bring happiness to the lives of others as well. This is a part of his way of life. When an Indian earns some money, he often sees that an older relative has enough warm clothing for a cold winter, even when he himself may need warm clothing, too.

We have a saying among the Cheyenne that is used to describe the old days: "We were all fat, or we were all thin." What does that tell you about the ways of the people?

Indian people do not want to lose this custom of sharing for the good of all. We believe it is an important part of the Indian way that we should keep.

What We Do 5

Education

Suppose you were an Indian boy or girl in Montana in the early 1800's. Do you think you would lie awake in your buffalo robe bed in the mornings waiting for your mother to call you to breakfast? Would you hurry to eat and dress and rush out of the tipi to catch the school bus? Would you spend Monday through Friday in the schoolhouse?

Of course not. Indian children were busy learning all the time during their childhood on the plains. They were not in classrooms, though. No one attended classes at regular times, because no one kept time by hours. No one had a calendar hanging on a tipi wall. Time was marked by the sun. Months were marked off by seasons instead of periods of 30 or 31 days. This was really all the calendar anyone needed.

A boy or girl did not grow up ignorant, though. From the time a child could walk, he was learning what he'd need to know to become a helpful man or woman of his group. A boy learned to shoot a bow and arrow. He shot first at targets, then at small animals. If he killed small animals, they were added to the cooking pot at home. A boy learned to ride horses. He

47

took care of the family's horses. He learned the habits of wild animals, so that when he was a man he could provide food for his family. All the time he listened to the stories of his people, so that he knew their history and was proud of it. He took part in the dances and the singing. By the time a boy was 15 or 16, he was called a man. He was expected to take his place among the hunters and the warriors.

A girl, too, learned her place among her people. She learned to find the wild plants that the family could eat. she learned to take care of the meat brought in by the hunters. She learned to make clothing and tipi covers out of the hides of animals. She learned to decorate the clothing with colored porcupine quills or beads. Some girls learned how to find and use the medicines found in wild plants.

Boys and girls both learned that men and women worked together for the good of all the people. They learned that sharing what one had was the best of all ways to live.

This does not sound like "school," does it? Yet it was a kind of school. Young people grew up learning the things they needed to know, knowing where their place was, and knowing what their life's work would be.

Schools during the early reservation period

In modern times, the Indian people have had many problems in learning to make the best of the white man's schools. Now, though, even the oldest Indians know that school is very important to their young people, but when Indian schools were first started, many Indian people did not want their children to go. When you hear their reasons, you will understand why.

When the Indian people were first put on reservations, the United States government leaders decided that Indians had to learn to become like white people. Most white people could not see that there was much good at all in the Indian way of life. The fastest way they could erase the Indian way of life was to take the children away from their homes and parents. Many children were made to live at schools far away from their homes for months and even years at a time. The children were taught to forget their Indian ways.

To make this clearer, imagine that someone of a stronger nation came to your state and snatched you and all the other children away from your families. Suppose that you and all the other children from your state—and children from other countries, too—were taken to one place that was far away from your families. You were confined to large buildings where many children lived together. You were given new names and made to dress alike—different from the way you dressed at home. Worst of all, you were never allowed to speak your own language, even though you did not under-stand the language you were supposed to speak.

This was a true story for many of the Indian people who are my age. I was sent away from home to a school in Idaho when I was just seven years old. I could not speak English, but I was not allowed to speak my own language. When I forgot and spoke in my own Northern Cheyenne language, I was spanked. For several years I did not see my own family. I lived at the school, which was called a boarding school.

Do you think there was much happiness in this school? No. There was very little to make an Indian child happy in these early boarding schools. Most of us did not learn very well because we were so homesick. Finally, many of us found that even when we did go home, we had forgotten our own language. We could not talk to our parents and grandparents. We were not happy at school and we were not happy at home. We did not fit anywhere. We were not white men nor were we Indians any longer.

Schools today

Nowadays, most of the boarding schools are closed. There is just one government boarding school for Indians left in Montana. It is mainly for children who have no homes to go to. Some of the churches run boarding schools for Indian children. These are private schools. In the past, the church schools were the only ones on some reservations, although now there are public schools for all.

Some of the reservations still have dormitories for children to live in while they go to high school. Many families live miles from a high school and the distance would be too much for bus travel each day. Many times it is so hard for an Indian boy or girl to go to high school that he drops out of school.

At first, in all the schools, the Indian children had the same problem of not knowing enough English to learn to read books written in English. Many children spent one year in the first grade learning to speak English, and then another year learning to read. Some children dropped out of school after a very few years because they could not keep up with the English language.

This is still true for many Indian children. However, with radio and television on the reservation, Indian children hear much more English than in the past. In fact, now most older Indian people are afraid that the Indian languages will be forgotten! Some are trying hard to be sure that Indian children can speak their own language as well as English.

Older people are also teaching many of the young people the good ways of the old time Indians. Some are teaching old songs, old stories, and old dances.

Some of us have learned to be proud of the kinds of arts and crafts that our people did in the past. In the schools and at home, Indian designs are being used by many people. Some of our young girls have learned the old ways of making moccasins decorated with beads. They find that beadwork can be sold at a good price to many people!

So, you see, the Indian people have come in a circle with their schools. First there was the school that was learning by doing. There was listening to wise old men and women, growing up to become proud warriors and hunters.

Then came the bad years of being forced to be like white men, of going to schools that tried to make Indians forget everything Indian.

Now most schools help us be proud to be Indian. We learn the ways of the white man, but we want to be Indians, too. It is important that each person knows both cultures well enough that he can choose from each what is best for him as a person. We do not all need to be alike, but we need to choose for ourselves and to be proud of who we are.

Religious Beliefs and Practices

The Pilgrims came to Plymouth Colony to worship God in their own way. The Pilgrims did not want anyone to tell them how they must carry on their church services. Other groups of people came from Europe to the North American continent for the same reason. This reason was freedom of religion. Freedom of religion was so important to the early settlers that when they wrote their Constitution, they wrote down that anyone in the whole land could worship God in any way he chose.

What about the Indian people that the Europeans found on the new continent when they arrived? Did the settlers think that freedom of religion was important to them, too? Let us think about the question a bit.

To the Europeans, many of the Indian's ways seemed different and strange. At that time, anyone whose ideas and way of life were different was considered a savage, and people would not consider trying to learn from them. Because of that attitude, and because of the differences in language, the Europeans rarely bothered to find out what the Indians believed. They did see that the Indian way of worship did not include singing hymns (at least not the way Europeans sang hymns!). The Indians did not have special buildings called churches.

But the Indians had other ways of worship. They had a strong faith in God and that faith was important in everything they did.

Worship of God, known to the Indians as the Great Spirit, was an everyday, common way of living. The early Plains Indians tried to live with God all the time. They believed God was in everything. All the earth was a holy place. Therefore, everything on the earth, under it, or above it, was sacred. They

SB

believed that they were always in the presence of God. All of the Plains Indian people prayed to God for His help in anything they did, in every move they made. They believed God was merciful and that He loved His people. They sang songs to God in praise of Him. They carried out ceremonies and dances in His honor. They thanked Him every day. There was no Sunday on the Indian calendar of seasons. Every day was God's day.

Missionaries, preachers and priests

The white men did not think these ways were right. For this reason, many missionaries, preachers, and priests went out among the Indian people to teach them the white man's religion.

The early priests and missionaries did not bother to find out that the Indians' beliefs were really a lot like their own. To the shocked white men, the dances were an unheard-of way of praising God. To them, the drums sounded weird and savage. To them, the Indian songs were not hymns!

Quickly, the early white religious teachers began to change the ways of the Indian. The missionaries built churches and schools on or near the reservations. They began to preach and teach, especially to the Indian children.

The missionaries have been successful, for many of the Indian people have forgotten that once they also had a very good religion of their own. They have forgotten that they were once all one group in their worship of God. Now they have become divided in their beliefs. They now believe in the ways of one church group or another. They are not together in their worship. Sometimes this division makes it hard for them to work for the good of all.

Even though the churches may have divided the Indian people among themselves, there has been much good done, too. Missionaries taught the Indians how to raise crops. They brought in medical care for the Indians who caught white men's diseases. They built homes and schools for Indian children. They have found jobs for Indian men and women. They often have helped the Indian people when there seemed to be no one else to care.

Religious practices today

There are still many different churches on the reservations. These churches are all doing what they think is the best thing for the Indian people.

Yet, some of our ways of worship and our ceremonies are still alive. Even young people take part. Some of our people think there is much good in the Indian way of worship, even for modern Indians. They make some of the old Indian ways of worship a part of their religious life. They think there is no need for Indians to be pulled this way and that by the white man's churches.

All of us, Indian and non-Indian alike, agree that one of the most important things religion should teach is that all people must be concerned for each other. They must worship God in their own ways. In our Indian religion, we pray for one another and for all people. We try to keep close to God and to the earth. We try to live each day in a good way.

Work

One of the hardest things for the Indian people to learn has been how to get and keep regular jobs.

Imagine, if you can, an Indian man in the days of hunting times. Would he say to himself, "Well, I'd like to be a book-keeper for the rest of my life?" Would he leave his tipi each morning at a regular time, arrive at his "job" at eight o'clock in the morning, work all day counting buffalo robes, and then at five o'clock, close his books and go to his tipi?

Or would a young woman start a small shop where she would go each day to make and sell moccasins?

Or would a man who was a skilled hunter start a cafe where he would prepare and sell buffalo steaks?

These ideas would have been silly for the Indian people in old times. My people had no word for "job." As for work, there was plenty of that! It was not a "job" that was carried out so that the family would have money. Work was hunting. Hunting furnished food and materials for clothing and shelter. Work was preparing that food for future use. Work was preparing the hides of animals so that they could be used.

There were no special hours to carry on these activities. When buffalo were found, hunting and preparing meat and hides was an around-the-clock "job" for everyone to do. Even the children helped. They herded the extra horses, or guarded the drying meat so that magpies and dogs would not carry it off.

Then, when the work of hunting was done, there was time for resting or visiting. There was time to make war to get new horses. There was time to drive other groups of hunters off the hunting grounds.

It is true that some Indian men and women might have special work to do. The medicine men, for example, would act as doctors for the wounded and sick among the people. Such men, and sometimes women, would trade their healing skills for meat, robes, or horses.

55

Some men might be especially good at making weapons. They would make bows and arrows or spears in exchange for meat. A woman who was very good at making moccasins or robes might make articles of clothing for others besides her own family. Nearly all the people, though, learned all the skills necessary to keep themselves alive. They really "made a living," as we now call it.

Work during the early reservation period

When the Indian people were put on reservations late in the 1800's, their greatest problem was how to keep themselves alive when there were no buffalo or other animals to hunt. No one knew about jobs. No one knew anything about making a living without hunting.

For a time, Indian hunters were hired by the Army as scouts or guides or policemen. The need for such people did not last long, and even these few men were soon without money. The United States government found that the Indian groups had to be supported by gifts of food and clothing. Such gifts barely kept the people alive. Indeed, many children and older people died of starvation during this bad time.

Some families tried farming, but the soil on the reservations was poor. Since the land was poor and the people didn't know anything about the white man's way of farming, this was not a success.

Some of the Indian people sold their land to buy food and clothing. When the money from the land was gone, these families had nothing, not even their land.

Work today

How is it now among the Indian people? Have the Indians learned that a job is something that each person must plan and work at? I wish I could answer "yes" to these questions. The truth is that most of my people still find it hard to carry out a life plan of work.

Most of the seven reservations in Montana are very small and very crowded. There is little within the reservations to support so many people. There is some ranching, farming, lumbering, and mining. But there is not enough work to furnish jobs for very many men or women.

Many of our young men and women go away from the reservations and even away from Montana. They learn a trade or go to school or to the Army. They are often very homesick for the lands of home. It is especially hard for them because Indian people like to be together. We enjoy our own families and friends. We consider all members of our group as friends and even family. Only on the reservation do we feel truly at home.

Some of our young people find they are unable to stay away from their reservation homes. They come back, only to find there is no work for them. These young people are caught in the middle of a big problem. They want to work. They need to work. But they do not want to go away because they need something of Indian life to hold to.

You can imagine what it would be like if half of all the adults in your town were unemployed and were told that the only way they had a chance of getting a job would be to go to a foreign country like Germany, Russia, or China. What do you think your family would do? How would you feel? A few young people would go willingly, but many more would want to stay near home, with their own people, their own way of life.

That is the way Indian people feel when they are forced to leave the reservation to get jobs. When they go to a big city where the people live very differently and have different ideas, they feel the same way you might feel if you were forced to live in a foreign country.

Many people are trying to help with this problem. Some have found steady, year-'round work for Indians on the reservations. Small factories on several reservations offer regular paying jobs for workers. More jobs in offices and schools are being given to Indian people. There are more and more places for Indians to get training for jobs. Some day perhaps all the jobs on the reservations will be filled by Indian people themselves.

Something is being done to help the Indians who are away from the reservations, too. All-Indian clubs are being formed in many cities and colleges. Indian workers and students may get together to talk over problems. They may even try to keep alive some of their Indian customs. These clubs help the Indians to have pride in being Indians. Even when he is working at a day-to-day job to support his family, each Indian is part of an Indian group. He does not feel alone. He is happier even though he is earning a living away from his home reservation. He can put his skills and training to use in a job, and still be an Indian.

Indian men and women can learn to do any kind of work if they are given a chance. Indians have proven to be very good at certain kinds of work which require patience, attention to detail, or lots of nerve. But whatever their jobs, these workers have something "extra" to give that we do not want them to forget! That is the Indian's concern for others of the human race. Indian people do not want to get so interested in "making a living" that they forget some of the good ways of the past.

Dances and Ceremonies

Often, in Indian lands, you can hear drums beating. Probably you would not hear drums as often now as you would have in the old hunting days, but Indian people still like to sing and they like to dance.

Lafe

From the television, you would think that Indians dance only war dances.

This is not true. A very small number of our dances are war dances. We have many other kinds of dances. Let me tell you about an Indian social dance.

Social dances

Social dances are usually held on special occasions, such as around Christmas. They are often held in the winter because the people need the warmth and cheerfulness of getting together. Sometimes one or two men give the dance and invite the singers and drummers.

Nearly every reservation town has some kind of building which can be used as a dancing place. It might be a Quonset hut, a building made of logs, or a school gymnasium.

In the building, as the dance gets under way, the people seat themselves on benches placed around the area. As people come into the dance building, there is much talking and visiting. The children all attend the dances, too, although some of them are sure to fall asleep late in the evening!

There is a stir of excitement when the singers arrive! They carry with them a big bass drum, the kind you might see in a high school band. This drum is set carefully in the middle of the floor. The singers seat themselves on chairs around the drum. Each singer has a stick with padding on the end. With this stick, each will beat the drum and sing with the others. Sometimes there are as many as five to seven singers, all playing the same drum. (Do you see the singers in the picture above?)

The singers are very special among the Indian people. They are the men who know many of the old songs. They must try to keep the old songs alive by teaching them to younger men. A group of singers is often surrounded by small boys. These singers hope that some of the small boys will become good singers when they grow up. Often at home the grandparents or parents sing songs they want the children to learn. Most Indian people do not want their good Indian songs to be forgotten.

When the singers are ready, they will begin to tap out the drum beat on the edges of the drum. Soon they will begin to beat on the drum head. And then! Who can stay in his seat when the drum really begins to speak? The women sing the songs from the benches, or they may dance and sing, too. Their singing adds a high part to the men's voices. Soon the floor is full of dancers, men and boys, women and girls. The sounds of the drumming, singing, ringing of bells, and some-times shouting from the men fill the air.

If you will look carefully at the picture of the dancers below, you will see how the men and women dress. We men proudly wear the buckskin and beadwork made for us by a woman in the family. The bells are an important part of every man's costume, for as he dances, the bells keep time.

A really good dance costume is worth a great deal of money. We put the costume away carefully between dances. Some of the women and girls wear real buckskin dresses with heavy beadwork and fringe. Any woman who owns one of these dresses is very proud of it.

Indians of the old days wore their hair long. Since most of us nowadays wear our hair short, we have to wear false braids under our headbands.

The singers are very special among the Indian people. They are the men who know many different kinds of dances—dances for couples, round dances, and contest dances, which are full of shouting, stomping, and sudden stops in the music, as the singers try to trick the dancers!

There are many good things about our Indian dances. One good thing is that the whole family can take part. Even small children are taught to dance and to sing the old songs. Beautiful beaded costumes are often made for the children.

Second, beading and making buckskin costumes help our women keep alive the old arts of design. Each woman tries to be sure the designs she uses are the "right" ones, the designs used years ago by her own group.

A third good thing to come from the dances is the feeling of pride. Sometimes it is when we are together doing something that is really Indian that we are most proud of being Indian.

The pow-wow

Nearly every Plains Indian group has at least one pow-wow every summer. These are usually either two or three days long and consist of many traditional Indian dances and songs, and often a feast for the guests. These are usually held in an open area near the village where there is space for a large circle of benches surrounding the dance area, and plenty of room for the tipis, tents, and campers of the Indians from other tribes who come to visit and share the experience.

These pow-wows are not designed as entertainment for tourists, nor to make money, as some outsiders assume. Although everyone is welcome, they are Indian activities put on by Indians for Indians of their own and other tribes. They are an opportunity to enjoy together their traditional activities. There is no charge for attending a pow-wow since they are paid for by the local Indian people as a way of sharing their cultural activities. The host tribe furnishes the space, the drummers and singers, and enough tipi poles for all the guests who bring their tipis.

Many Indian families attend several different pow-wows every summer and bring along elaborate beaded costumes which they have made to wear while dancing.

The largest of the Plains Indian pow-wows is the "Crow Fair" which is held every August. It lasts five days and includes not only dancing and dance contests every afternoon and evening, but also giveaways, parades, and a rodeo. There are always more than 500 Indian families from all over the west camped on the pow-wow grounds. More than 150 of them stay in tipis.

Other ceremonies and dances

The Giveaway

In addition to the social dances and pow-wows, there are other times when a serious ceremony or dance will take place. These are held for special purposes. For instance, let us say a young man is a soldier and has returned safely from war. His family wants to show how grateful they are that he has returned. The family will arrange a dance with traditional honoring songs, and a giveaway in which they will give other people many gifts. In the old days, these gifts might have included horses, but nowadays not so many people have horses, so they give other gifts of value instead.

At the same time that the family conducts the giveaway, they will often give the young soldier a new name. He will be given a warrior's name. In honor of the new name, his family will furnish a great feast.

The Sun Dance

The greatest of serious occasions among some of the Plains Indians is the Sun Dance. Many people think this dance is given in honor of the Sun. This is not true. In fact, it is not even a "dance," but, rather, a serious religious ceremony. During this time, many prayers are said to thank God for all His blessings, for the earth and all of life.

One may vow to sponsor a Sun Dance because he has a special reason for giving thanks. His friends will help him to prepare the special place for the ceremony. Singers will come to sing the special Sun Dance songs to help the dancers.

The Sun Dance is a hard thing to do, as the men who take part in it must go without food and water for three days. At different times during the night and day, they dance lightly in one place. They blow on an eagle wing whistle. At other times they can rest.

The men who dance know they are doing it for all of the people. They know that the Indian people are praying with them. The dancers are not showing off, as some white people think. They are praying at all times during the four days. When the dance is over, the Indian people feel new and clear in their spirits.

Keeping the customs

Many Indian leaders think the Indian songs, dances, and ceremonies help their people, so they try to carry them on just as they have always been done. Sometimes this has been very difficult.

Just as the Indians were once not allowed to speak their own language, or to keep their own religion, they also were not allowed to continue any of their old ways of celebrating. For many years, Indian dances were not allowed on the reservations.

How did the Indians manage to keep their own customs alive? Some of the older Indians in each group in Montana taught the songs and dances in secret. It is true that many of the songs have been lost because they are forgotten. Many are known today, though. These songs and ceremonies are now taught again. The Indians are not afraid, now, that they will be punished for being Indians. Records and tape recordings have been made by the old, old Indians who remembered the songs and the ways of the ceremonies.

Some white people helped in keeping a record of the old ways. Long before the Indian people could read or write, white artists and writers put down the stories of some of the dances and ceremonies.

Now many of us of the Plains Indians think that keeping alive the real Indian songs, dances, and ceremonies will help the Indian people. They are something that the Indian people have that is really theirs. They are not borrowed from the white man. They belonged to the Indians long before Columbus set foot on the land that is now called America. Indians can be proud of their own ways of celebrating. They really enjoy talking together in their own language, dancing their own dances, and eating their own foods.

We hope these things from the old ways will continue so that Indians will always have some things to share that are really theirs. We can enjoy our Indian ways together. We can be proud to be Indians.

What We Hope For 6

The Indians once had a good life on the open plains. They enjoyed the freedom, hunting, and moving about. That life is now only a dream. It is a life that would be impossible in our modern world.

When the white man took over the land, the Indian was forced to change his way of life. The white people said, "There is nothing good about being an Indian. Forget your Indian ways as fast as you can and become as white people are."

To many of us Montana Indians, becoming as a white person is not always a good thing. A white person's ways of rushing about, of wanting more and more new things, of forgetting the earth and its beauty are not good ways. But there are good things in both Indian and white societies. Perhaps for Indians, a combination of the good things from both the white and Indian ways would be best.

Sitting Bull, a great Sioux Indian leader said, "Whenever you find anything good in the white man's world, pick it up and use it. If it is bad, drop it and leave it alone."

What are some of the things Indians hope for in combining white and Indian cultures?

1. We hope that all Indian boys and girls will finish school. We hope that all reservation schools can have Indian teachers, principals, and school boards. In these schools, Indian history should be taught so that Indian students will learn to be proud of their history and culture.

2. We hope that all Indian people who want to hold jobs can get the training they need for these jobs. Work and jobs are a part of everyone's life on earth. The Indian people know they must work for their share of the money and goods. They hope for a fair opportunity to earn their share.

3. We hope that, along with schools and jobs, we can live in a good Indian way. Of course, we cannot go back to the old free life, but there are many of the good ways that we can remember and use. Even the white men could use some of these ways!

It would be a good thing if all people followed the Indian way of being close to earth and to nature. Even in the cities, we need to remember that all life comes from the earth. Perhaps remembering this would help people to slow down. It would help us conserve the earth's resources.

It would also be good if all people would follow the old Indian way of doing a thing for the good of all the people. Indians once were proud of the acts of courage and generosity of everyone in their group.

4. We hope that Indian people will remember that bravery against all danger was an important part of old-time Indian life. Indians now need to have that bravery to face the dangers of modern life. Young people face many pressures to use drugs or alcohol, or to do other things that are harmful to themselves and others. They must think clearly and stand up for what they believe. It takes more courage to live in a good way now than it ever did in the old days.

5. Most important of all, we hope that all Indians can have pride in being Indian. On or off the reservation, we hope to be proud of being good American citizens.

Afterword

I have spoken many words about Plains Indian people. I have spoken of good things and bad things in our lives.

Perhaps the best time for all of us will come when all children learn to choose the very best from both the white and Indian worlds and make them their own.

—Vostaas (White Buffalo)